MODERN ROLE MODELS

John Cena

Robert Grayson

Mason Crest Publishers

Produced by OTTN Publishing in association with
21st Century Publishing and Communications, Inc.

MASON CREST PUBLISHERS INC.
370 Reed Road
Broomall, Pennsylvania 19008
(866) MCP-BOOK (toll free)
www.masoncrest.com

Printed in the United States of America.

First Printing

9 8 7 6 5 4 3 2 1

Library of Congress Cataloging-in-Publication Data

Grayson, Robert, 1951—
    John Cena / Robert Grayson.
      p. cm. — (Modern role models)
    Includes bibliographical references and index.
ISBN-13: 978-1-4222-0500-6 (hardcover) — ISBN-13: 978-1-4222-0787-1 (pbk.)
ISBN-10: 1-4222-0500-2 (hardcover)
 1. Cena, John—Juvenile literature. 2. Wrestlers—United States—Biography—Juvenile literature. 3. Motion picture actors and actresses—United States—Biography—Juvenile literature. I. Title.
GV1196.C46G73 2009
796.812092—dc22
[B]   2008020405

Publisher's note:
All quotations in this book come from original sources, and contain the spelling and grammatical inconsistencies of the original text.

CROSS-CURRENTS

In the ebb and flow of the currents of life we are each influenced by many people, places, and events that we directly experience or have learned about. Throughout the chapters of this book you will come across CROSS-CURRENTS reference boxes. These boxes direct you to a CROSS-CURRENTS section in the back of the book that contains fascinating and informative sidebars and related pictures. Go on. ▶▶

CONTENTS

1 Top of the World 5

2 Learning to Be Strong 11

3 Making of a Champion 17

4 Hitting the Big Time 27

5 Being the Best 37

Cross-Currents 46

Chronology 56

Accomplishments & Awards 58

Further Reading & Internet Resources 59

Glossary 60

Notes 61

Index 62

Picture Credits 64

About the Author 64

John Cena holds up his WWE World Championship belt. When he won the title in 2005, John—known as one of wrestling's hardest-working stars—decided to have a belt custom-made. The diamond-encrusted gold belt featured a spinning center plate. "I really wanted to take the WWE to another level," John said.

Top of the World

JOHN CENA MAY BE THE HARDEST-WORKING person in sports entertainment. John is always on the go—inside and outside the ring—with thriving careers as a pro wrestler, an actor, and a rap singer. Add to that his guest appearances, commercial endorsements, and charity work, and you can see why John likes to defeat his wrestling opponents quickly and move on.

John was everywhere in 2007—from the ring to the tennis court to U.S. military installations overseas, where he was boosting the morale of the nation's troops. Even his peers in the **squared circle** marvel at John's rigorous schedule, which includes taking on all challengers in the ring.

⇒ A BREAKOUT YEAR ⇐

John battled in the ring more than 200 times and won two championship titles in 2007. He was the WWE (World Wrestling

Entertainment) champion as well as the World Tag Team champion with Shawn Michaels.

In January 2007, John's action thriller *The Marine* was released on DVD after a successful run in movie theaters. The muscular 240-pound, 6'1" professional wrestling star showed action film fans that he could pack as much excitement on the movie screen as he could in the ring. In its first three months on rental shelves, the film took in $30 million. In addition, John kept busy writing hip-hop music in anticipation of releasing another CD. His first CD, 2005's *You Can't See Me*, had hit number 15 on the Billboard 200 charts. Regarding his **foray** into movies and music, John told WWE.com:

> **"I'm one that loves to take the bull by the horns. If something challenging comes along and it's something I feel like I could pull off, I'm going to try."**

Because he was making a name for himself as a triple threat—in the fields of professional wrestling, acting, and music—John was getting a lot of invitations to appear at red-carpet events all over the country.

⟫ KEEPING IT REAL ⟪

Fans were clamoring to see more of the **charismatic** athlete whose relentless training program had pushed him to the top of the wrestling world. What captivates fans most about this rural Massachusetts bodybuilder-turned-wrestler? John keeps it real. His dad, John Sr., says:

> **"What you see is the real John Cena. What you see is what you get. He doesn't play a role or take on a character. That's really him."**

CROSS-CURRENTS
To learn more about the system by which professional wrestlers are ranked, check out "The PWI 500." Go to page 46. ▶▶

Fans loved the real John Cena so much that they voted him Wrestler of the Year in 2007, an honor he had also won in 2006. The editors and writers of *Pro Wrestling Illustrated* ranked John the number one wrestler in the world in 2007, at the top of the PWI 500 list.

Outside the ring, John could be seen on television commercials for Subway restaurants. He also endorsed two signature collections of energy bars and drinks, produced by American Body Builders.

When WWE superfan Rick "Sign Guy" Achberger was a contestant on the top-rated game show *Deal or No Deal*, the show's producers

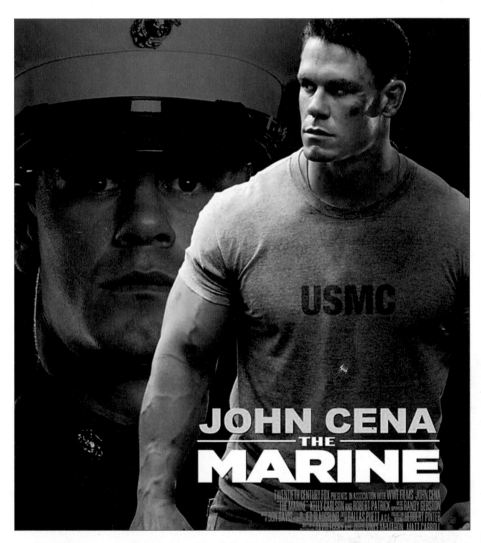

A publicity poster for *The Marine*. The 2006 action movie starred John Cena as an Iraq War vet whose wife, played by Kelly Carlson, is kidnapped by a gang of diamond thieves. The movie, though panned by critics, did reasonably well at the box office and was quite popular as a DVD release.

surprised him by inviting John Cena and fellow pro wrestler Bobby Lashley to cheer him on. John also appeared with other WWE pro wrestlers on an episode of the popular game show *Family Feud*.

Playing off John's love of cars, ABC cast him in the reality series *Fast Cars & Superstars: The Gillette Young Guns Celebrity Race*. Showing the same intensity on the racetrack as he shows in the ring, John handled the corners at Lowe's Motor Speedway in Concord, North Carolina, like a NASCAR pro. He stayed in the competition right through the show's final episode, coming in third overall.

CROSS-CURRENTS

Interested in learning more about one of John Cena's favorite hobbies outside the wrestling ring? Read "A Car Guy." Go to page 47. ▶▶

⟫ ALWAYS WILLING TO HELP ⟪

With a heart as big as his biceps, John played tennis at the 12th annual Arthur Ashe Kids' Day at the USTA Billie Jean King National Tennis Center in Flushing, New York, to raise money for inner-city kids; helped bring a smile to critically ill children through the Make-A-Wish Foundation; and pursued his personal mission—and that of the WWE—to let U.S. troops overseas know how much the nation appreciates their service and sacrifice. John visited with soldiers at Camp Speicher in Tikrit, Iraq, and other U.S. bases.

John and fellow pro wrestler Batista, together with WWE diva Ashley Massaro, made time to travel to Chicago's West Side to help renovate a structurally unsound brick house for a disadvantaged family. The trio of WWE stars appeared on *Extreme Makeover: Home Edition*. Besides pitching in to refurbish the house, they brought gifts for the family.

⟫ SOME SERIOUS SETBACKS ⟪

Despite reaching some new heights in 2007, John had a few lows as well. After Shawn Michaels and John won the World Tag Team Championship in January, Michaels turned on John in a 10-team Battle Royal. He threw John out of the ring during the match, costing the team the title.

John's biggest blow was a serious injury he suffered while executing a hip toss in a match against Ken Kennedy on October 1, 2007. Though John finished the match and won, he had torn his **pectoral muscle**. He needed emergency surgery. Although the

U.S. Army journalists prepare to film an interview with John Cena at Camp Speicher, near Tikrit, Iraq, December 2007. John has traveled to Iraq, Afghanistan, and other countries where American soldiers are stationed as part of the WWE's "Tribute to the Troops" tours. He believes it is important to let the soldiers know the country appreciates their service.

operation went well, John would not be able to return to the ring for at least seven months, and possibly a year.

Because John couldn't defend his championship, the WWE stripped him of his title. As 2007 was drawing to a close, John had no titles and was recovering from a very severe injury that would require months of strenuous **rehabilitation**. His professional wrestling career hung in the balance.

Today John Cena packs 240 pounds of rock-hard muscle on a 6'1" frame. But he was a scrawny youngster who suffered frequent bullying. At age 13, John decided that he'd had enough and began lifting weights. Since that time he has been working out with single-minded dedication.

Learning to Be Strong

JOHN CENA'S DAD, JOHN SR., LOVED PROFES-sional wrestling and found that watching it on TV with his sons was a great way for them to bond. "It's the only reason I got cable," he says. The family's love for professional wrestling turned into a very successful career in the squared circle for John Jr.

Jonathan Felix Anthony Cena Jr. was born on April 23, 1977, in West Newbury, Massachusetts. He was the second son of John Cena Sr. and his wife, Carol. John Jr. has four brothers: Dan, Matt, Steve, and Sean.

⇛ A YOUNG FAN ⇚

John Cena grew up watching Hulk Hogan, Ultimate Warrior, and André the Giant. But John's dad never thought he'd be watching his son in the ring one day. John Cena Sr. recalled:

> **"If you would have told me that my son was going to be a professional wrestler, I would have said you were nuts."**

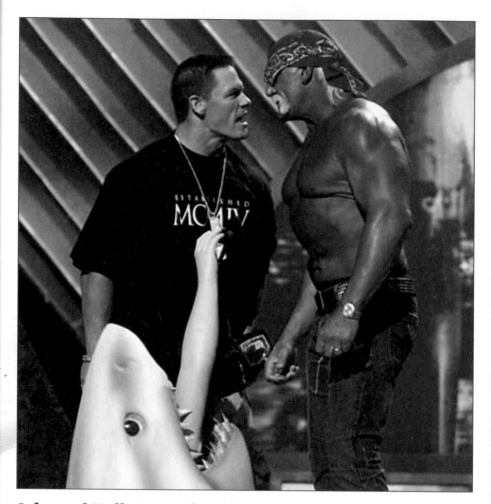

John and Hulk Hogan ham it up at the 2005 Teen Choice Awards, Universal City, California, August 14, 2005. When John was growing up, he was a huge fan of wrestling, and the Hulkster was one of the sport's biggest stars. Hulk made his wrestling debut in 1977, the year John Cena was born.

John Sr. recalls that John built a miniature wrestling ring and had action figures of pro wrestlers:

❝He made a Championship wrestling belt out of paper, and still has the original belt he made hanging in his home. He had a Tag Team Championship belt as well.❞

The Cena boys would wrestle at home—downstairs on the concrete basement floor, upstairs in the house, and outside on the lawn. John had another passion growing up—rap music. He dressed like rap stars of the day, with baggy pants and wingtip shoes. The kids he was growing up with, however, liked rock music and T-shirts.

A scrawny youngster, John was picked on at school because of his fashion and music choices. Even worse, he was bullied and punched. One day, when he was 13 years old, John had had enough. He asked his dad to buy him a set of weights.

⇛ BUILDING MUSCLES ⇚

John has been working out ever since. At 15, he decided to join a gym. Along the way the **taunts** from bullies stopped, as John's muscles began to show and he became a football player while attending high school at Cushing Academy in Ashburnham, Massachusetts.

John applied to 60 colleges and was accepted into 58 of them. He chose to attend Springfield College, a National Collegiate Athletic Associ-ation (NCAA) Division III school located in Massachusetts, where he was an outstanding football player.

CROSS-CURRENTS

If you would like to learn more about bodybuilding competitions, check out "The Sport of Bodybuilding." Go to page 48. ▶▶

⇛ A STANDOUT IN COLLEGE ⇚

John became a star on Springfield College's football team. The talented athlete played center, an offensive line position. In his senior year, he was named team captain and won All-American honors. Throughout his college football career, he continued working out with weights while practicing with the football team. John's football coach at Springfield, Mike DeLong, was impressed with the future wrestling star's dedication:

"Two things I remember about John. He's an out-standing person and he has a tremendous work ethic. A very positive person, he worked hard."

John never missed a single practice or game during his college play-ing days.

John graduated from Springfield College in 1999 with a degree in exercise physiology. He headed to California to pursue a career in bodybuilding. He landed a job at Gold's Gym in Venice, California, coaching people who were just as passionate about working out and bodybuilding as he was.

⟫ FROM BODYBUILDING TO WRESTLING ⟪

One day John was talking to a member at the gym, and the man mentioned that he was training to be a professional wrestler at a nearby wrestling academy. John decided to check out the school himself. Once there, John was sold. He enrolled in Ultimate University, run by Ultimate Pro Wrestling (UPW). John told the *Baltimore Sun*:

> **"Wrestling was always so secretive about how you [break in]. When somebody told me that there was a school to go to for becoming a wrestler, I was hooked."**

John was in the ring by early 2000, wrestling under the **moniker** "the Prototype." At first, John didn't tell his dad about his decision to become a wrestler. John Sr. recalls:

CROSS-CURRENTS

John's father became involved in wrestling around the same time his son did. To learn more, read "Like Son, Like Father." Go to page 49. ▶▶

> **"He didn't tell me he was trying out. He just called one day and said, 'Dad, I got a second job.' I said, 'What are you doing?' and he said, 'I'm a professional wrestler.' So I flew to California to see for myself."**

In April 2000, John won the UPW Championship—his first wrestling title. He held the title for just under a month, but still managed to grab the attention of promoters of the World Wrestling Federation.

In 2001 the World Wrestling Federation, or WWF (later known as the WWE), came calling. The WWF was one of the largest professional wrestling promotion organizations in the world at the time. It presented wrestling matches in major sports arenas and on network television. The WWF signed John to a developmental contract, which meant he would continue to train and hone his skills as a wrestler.

Wrestling is an enormously popular form of entertainment. Fans pack large arenas to watch their favorite stars perform. But to reach the big time, a wrestler must first pay his dues. After being signed to a developmental contract by the World Wrestling Federation, John Cena began honing his skills in a small regional league, Ohio Valley Wrestling.

Then, if he proved good enough, the WWF would get him matches in major arenas with big-name opponents.

⇒ EARLY SUCCESS ⇐

His first assignment for the WWF was to wrestle as part of Ohio Valley Wrestling (OVW), a small regional wrestling league. He continued to use the moniker Prototype and also wrestled as Mr. P. While with the OVW, John earned two titles: Heavyweight Champion; and, with Rico Constantino, Southern Tag Team Champion. By the beginning of 2002, the WWF was ready to bring John to the big time. Soon, youngsters everywhere would be turning on the television and watching his exploits in the ring—just as he had watched other wrestlers years ago with his own dad.

In 2002 the WWE was looking for a chiseled wrestler with a clean-cut, All-American image, and John Cena fit the bill. He got his first big break on June 27 of that year, when he climbed into the ring with Kurt Angle for a match broadcast on the WWE's *Smackdown!*

Making of
a Champion

AS THE DOMINANT PLAYER ON THE WORLD
wrestling scene, the WWF was poised to introduce new
talent in the ring. John Cena's timing seemed perfect.
The WWF was searching for a wrestler with his character, drive, and exceptional athletic ability, a clean-cut,
All-American boy with bulging muscles and an easy
smile. John was someone the fans could cheer on.

John had the added attraction of being a very eligible bachelor
(he still is). That helped draw women of all ages to his rapidly growing fan base.

Shortly before John made it big in the ring, the WWF decided to
change its name to World Wrestling Entertainment (WWE) to avoid
conflict and confusion with an environmental organization called
the World Wildlife Fund, also referred to by the initials WWF. In
the spring of 2002, WWE chairman Vince McMahon gave some
of wrestling's rising young stars a pep talk. He told the **aspiring**

wrestling pros that they would have to earn their place alongside the ring's greats. Doing that would require them to take an aggressive approach in all their matches.

John took McMahon's words to heart. When Kurt Angle, one of the WWE's biggest stars, challenged all comers to a match, John stepped forward and took him up on the offer. In wrestling circles, Angle was known as an accomplished athlete. He had been a wrestling star in high school and college. He had won two NCAA Division I wrestling championships and a gold medal in wrestling at the 1996 Olympics in Atlanta. He was well respected, smooth in the ring, and utterly feared by his opponents.

⇒ JOHN'S DEBUT ON *SMACKDOWN!* ⇐

John's first live televised match for the WWE was broadcast on June 27, 2002, during one of the WWE's most popular television programs, *Smackdown!* The match pitted him against Kurt Angle. John didn't know what to expect, but he was ready to throw everything he had at the WWE veteran star. John wanted to make the most of this chance—and he did. As the two battled in the ring, John was handling the seasoned wrestler quite well; he was actually controlling the match. He showed fans that he was tough, that he was **savvy**, and that he belonged in the ring with Kurt Angle. John battled Angle for a while, but what impressed fans the most was that John managed to withstand a painful ankle lock submission hold and then kick out of an Angle Slam, one of his opponent's most devastating moves.

CROSS-CURRENTS
If you would like a better understanding of professional wrestling finishing moves, read "The Signature Move." Go to page 50. ▶▶

John was ultimately pinned by Angle, but the viewers liked how the newcomer handled himself in the ring. They wanted to see more of this talented young wrestler with a lot of heart. John got more televised matches, including one on the July 11, 2002, episode of *Smackdown!* During that event, he teamed up with one of professional wrestling's biggest names, the Undertaker.

John and the Undertaker—all 6'10½" and 305 pounds of him—were taking on John's old foe, Kurt Angle, and another big-name wrestler, Chris Jericho. John and the Undertaker won the match. Again, fans liked what they saw, and John continued working his way up the ranks in the WWE. He went on tour for the WWE, appearing in arenas throughout the United States and Europe. John was no

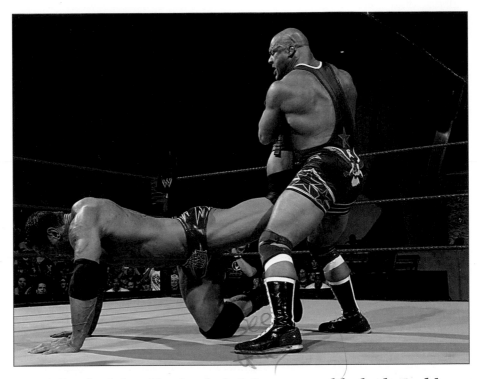

Kurt Angle (standing) administers an ankle lock. In his WWE television debut, John Cena impressed wrestling fans by refusing to succumb to Angle's painful submission hold. In the end, however, Angle pinned the newcomer. But John's gutsy performance against one of the WWE's toughest brawlers signaled that he would be heard from in the future.

longer going by the name Prototype (which played on his angular, machinelike moves). But he didn't have a gimmick, something the fans could look forward to seeing him perform every time he entered the ring.

GETTING A GIMMICK

In professional wrestling it's the gimmicks that set wrestlers apart. Fans respond to wrestlers' gimmicks—a particular style of dress, a distinctive way of speaking, an outrageous color scheme, a wacky hairstyle, even an unusual facial expression. These gimmicks become part of the wrestling culture and give the wrestlers fan appeal.

JOHN CENA

In 2002 European fans got to see live WWE action when the *RAW* Rebellion Tour stopped in Finland, Northern Ireland, and England. John Cena joined other WWE stars—including Kurt Angle, Chris Benoit, Edge, Booker T, and Brock Lesnar—on *RAW* Rebellion. It was during this tour that John's gift for freestyle rapping emerged as a potential gimmick in the ring.

John actually did have something that could be used as a gimmick, but nobody realized it. In his early days with the WWE, he would do freestyle rap backstage before his matches to relieve tension. Nobody gave this a second thought because most wrestlers have some routine they follow to keep them loose before matches.

In mid-October 2002, John went on the *RAW* Rebellion Tour. *RAW* is a television wrestling program, and the *RAW* Rebellion Tour was a live, arena version of the TV show, featuring many of the same wrestlers. The tour staged matches in major cities throughout the world, including Helsinki, Finland; Belfast, Northern Ireland; and Manchester and Sheffield, England. In England, the wrestlers took a bus between cities. After the last event, many of them were sitting in the back of the bus talking when a hip-hop session broke out.

⇒ RAPPING AND RHYMING ⇐

All the wrestlers were taking turns rhyming and doing hip-hop. When John's turn came, he drew on his childhood love for the hip-hop sound. Freestyling for more than 10 minutes, John kept his audience of wrestlers entertained and amazed with his **improvisational** rap. One rhyme followed another, and John felt totally at ease sharing his love for rap music with his fellow wrestlers.

As it happened, many members of the WWE's promotional and creative team were sitting in the front of the bus, and they heard John freestyling as well. By the time the wrestlers and the creative team were flying back to the United States, plans were already in the works to use John's freestyling talents as his gimmick in the ring.

John would adopt the image of a rap singer and use rhymes to taunt his opponents. John loved the idea because he was always a big rap music fan, and the gimmick allowed him to be himself. In an interview with *Men's Fitness* magazine, John said:

> **"My character is me. I'm one of the lucky ones. I get to be myself. When I'm out there in front of 20,000 people, I turn the volume up. But it's still me."**

Less than a week after he returned from the *RAW* Rebellion Tour, he made another appearance on *Smackdown!* It was a special Halloween episode of the show, and John came out dressed like rap star

Vanilla Ice. In the ring, he did freestyle rap for Stephanie McMahon, the daughter of the WWE's chairman. A week later he started coming into the ring before each of his matches dressed like a rap star and freestyling.

Through rap, he would either make fun of his current opponent or challenge another wrestler. Like many rappers, he would wear baseball caps and sports jerseys—usually throwback jerseys.

John decided to use the number 54 on all the jerseys he wore in the ring. Fans didn't realize it, but 54 was the number John had worn as a football player during his playing days at Springfield College. Though John would wear jerseys from various teams when he stepped into the ring, he liked to wear jerseys from his hometown favorites—major league baseball's Boston Red Sox, the NFL's New England Patriots, and the NBA's Boston Celtics. As John's rapping became more popular with fans, the WWE starting producing souvenir merchandise with the number 54 on it.

CROSS-CURRENTS

Read "The Wrestler and the Hip-Hop Artist" to find out about John's collaboration with his cousin, rapper Tha Trademarc. Go to page 51. ▶▶

Meanwhile, John was taking note of which of his raps fans were responding to, and he started looking toward putting out a CD of his best work. In a related gimmick, John began entering the ring with a heavy bicycle chain and lock around his neck. His fans started calling themselves members of the "Chain Gang."

⟫ MAKING HIS MOVE ⟪

In early 2003 John decided to make his move and try to claim the highly **coveted** WWE Championship. By now John was a regular on *Smackdown!* So he challenged WWE champ Brock Lesnar with weekly freestyle raps daring the champ to wrestle him. It was during his attempt to get Lesnar in the ring that John unveiled his now-famous signature or finishing move. Called the FU, or Fireman's Carry PowerSlam, the move shows off John's tremendous power and strength. After he battles an opponent and wears him out, he lifts his rival in the air and puts him facedown on his shoulders, like a fireman carrying a victim out of a burning building. John then body slams him, back first, onto the hard wrestling canvas and pins him. John has even done this move on two opponents at the same time. He developed the move as a takeoff of Lesnar's finishing move, called the F5, and claimed it was a better move then Lesnar's.

By early 2003 John Cena had developed a highly popular pre-match routine. Wearing a sports jersey from one of his favorite teams, John would enter the ring with a heavy chain and lock around his neck (his fans began referring to themselves as members of the "Chain Gang"). He would proceed to launch into a rap that taunted his rivals.

John Cena is blessed with Herculean strength. Here he lifts *two* opponents on his shoulders to execute his trademark finishing move, the FU, or Fireman's Carry PowerSlam. Opponents on the receiving end of the devastating move are slammed, back first, onto the canvas. Before they know what hit them, John usually has his opponents pinned.

Lesnar wanted nothing to do with John's move and refused to battle the upstart no matter how much he taunted him with rap lyrics. But John found another way to get his shot at the champ. He entered a contender tournament on April 17, 2003. The winner of that tournament won the right to fight Lesnar. John defeated long-time wrestling superstar Chris Benoit in a grueling battle and got his title match.

At Backlash 2003, a major wrestling pay-per-view event produced by the WWE on April 27, 2003, the champ could no longer avoid John Cena. He had to wrestle John for the title. Many of John's fans were on hand for the event, since the match was being staged in Worcester, Massachusetts, close to John's hometown of West Newbury.

➤ FALLING SHORT ◄

The battle between John and the champ was fierce. John realized that this was an excellent chance for him to grab his first WWE title. But it was not to be, as Lesnar finally defeated the top contender after 15 minutes of nonstop action. The champ was able to finish John off with his famed F5 move. Still, no one could deny John's determination, and he was not discouraged by the defeat. He continued to take on an array of tough and challenging opponents, winning many of these matches, and he kept on impressing promoters.

John told *Men's Fitness* magazine in an interview:

> **"I'm not afraid to fail. A lot of guys get shook up about doing things wrong. I get shook up about not trying. . . ."**

So despite his loss to Lesnar, John was not defeated. Rather, he became even more determined to win a championship belt. He set his sights on two big upcoming wrestling events—the Royal Rumble and WrestleMania XX.

Fans applaud John Cena, who holds up his championship belt after a successful defense. John battled the top grapplers in the WWE for two years before he finally realized his dream of winning a title. He would quickly discover that holding on to a belt is just as difficult as getting one in the first place.

Hitting the Big Time

JOHN CENA'S TIME HAD COME. HE HAD NEARLY won the WWE Championship in 2003. He desperately wanted that belt. John started off 2004 by entering the Royal Rumble on January 25 in Philadelphia. In a Royal Rumble, 30 wrestlers enter the ring and battle for the title. The winner is the last man standing.

For a pro wrestler to be eliminated in a Royal Rumble, he must be thrown out over the top rope and both his feet must hit the ground. John made it to the final six contestants before being eliminated by the WWE U.S. champion, a giant of a man called Big Show, who weighed 500 pounds and stood 7'1". John was upset by the defeat, and a feud began between him and Big Show. Six weeks of frustration came to an end on March 14, 2004, in Madison Square Garden in New York City. There John met Big Show in the ring at WrestleMania XX.

CROSS-CURRENTS

For the history of one of the most famous and important pro wrestling events, read "WrestleMania." Go to page 52. ▶▶

A promotional poster for WrestleMania XX, held March 14, 2004, at New York City's Madison Square Garden. John Cena's match against Big Show is advertised in the far left column, second from top. Throughout the match, John would apply relentless pressure, finally finishing off Big Show with the FU move. The victory gave John the U.S. Championship, his first WWE title.

John wasted no time assaulting the massive man. Early in the match, John scoop-slammed the 500-pound giant twice, and he kept up a fierce attack. Finally, John lifted Big Show up and slammed him down with his signature FU move, pinning the U.S. champion and winning the title. It was John's first title with World Wrestling Entertainment.

Titles are not easy to hold on to in professional wrestling. As soon as a wrestler wins a title, challengers line up to take it away. John successfully defended the U.S. Championship title for nearly four months. The end came on July 8, 2004, during a televised episode of *Smackdown!* At that time Kurt Angle—a John Cena rival who was then the general manager of *Smackdown!*—**alleged** that John had committed a rules violation. Angle offered no proof, but he used his power as general manager to strip John of his hard-won title.

➤ REGAINING THE TITLE ◄

But John never felt sorry for himself. He continued wrestling and started a bruising best-of-five series with Booker T. The prize was the U.S. Championship title. Fast and extremely talented, the 6'3", 250-pound Booker T was an experienced opponent—he had been a professional wrestler since 1989. The series started at SummerSlam '04 in Toronto, Canada, in August 2004. With the series tied at two wins apiece, the tiebreaker was set for October 3, 2004, at No Mercy, another annual WWE pay-per-view event. At the 2004 version of No Mercy—which was staged at the Meadowlands in East Rutherford, New Jersey—John defeated Booker T. By winning his third match in the best-of-five series, John laid claim to the U.S. Championship for a second time.

John Cena (on top) tries to break down his opponent. Throughout 2004 and early 2005, John kept up a hectic schedule, wrestling frequently in the United States, filming a movie in Australia, and recording tracks for his first rap CD, *You Can't See Me.*

In a stunning development, however, John lost his title just a week later to a wrestler making his debut on *Smackdown!* That wrestler was 5'10", 200-pound Carlito, known as the Caribbean Cool. John was still recovering from his tough series with Booker T, but he made no excuses for the loss. Instead, he began to train hard to win the title back.

➤ MAKING A MOVIE ⬅

During this time, John also **embarked** on an acting career. By chance, the script for a movie called *The Marine* came his way. The script had been written for Stone Cold Steve Austin, a longtime big-name professional wrestler. But Austin and the WWE had parted ways by the time the film was ready to be made. WWE officials were looking for a new star with the right look and build to play the lead role of John Triton, a daring former member of the U.S. Marine Corps. They felt that John Cena would be perfect for the role. In the movie, John's character returns home from Iraq after being discharged from the military, only to see his wife, played by Kelly Carlson, kidnapped by a gang of murderous thieves. He tracks them down and rescues her.

John was determined to keep up his rigorous schedule of wrestling appearances even during the filming. However, the movie was being shot in Australia, and most of John's wrestling bouts were in the United States. So he flew back and forth from his bouts to the movie set every week for more than three and a half months. Sometimes the commute took 18 hours.

The film's director, John Bonito, raved about John Cena's dedication in an interview with *Toro* magazine. "John is a director's dream," Bonito said. "He will do anything it takes." Kelly Carlson, John's costar, concurred. "[John Cena] has a strong work ethic," she told the *Los Angeles Daily News*, "he's open to learning and he has no attitude."

Until he got the film role, John had no acting experience and had never taken an acting lesson. When the movie was released, he told the *Baltimore Sun*:

> **❝I got about a month and a half of acting lessons before I hit the set, and had an acting coach with me on the set every day. It was just as much preparation as I could possibly cram in. ❞**

John Cena, as former U.S. Marine John Triton, scrambles to escape an explosion in a scene from *The Marine*. John did most of his own stunts for the 2006 movie. However, some movie critics complained that John did not display the same commanding presence on screen that he showed in the wrestling ring.

With a crew cut, a square jaw, and a terrific physique, John looked every inch a Marine. And by doing most of his own stunts in the movie, John stayed right in the middle of the action.

For John, the biggest difference between making movies and appearing in the ring almost every day is that there are no second takes in wrestling: No matter what happens, the match goes on. Though filming on *The Marine* started in 2004 and continued through the early part of 2005, the movie was not released in theaters until October 2006.

CROSS-CURRENTS

To learn about other pro wrestlers who have made their mark in movies, check out "Wrestlers on the Big Screen." Go to page 53. ▶▶

⟫ MAKING MUSIC, TOO ⟪

By the time *The Marine* hit theaters, John was familiar with promotional tours, both in wrestling and in the music business. With the help of hip-hop artist Tha Trademarc, John had put out his first rap CD in May 2005. The CD, titled *You Can't See Me*, spent more than four months on the Billboard Top 200 chart. It contained many of the rhymes John used in the ring.

Meanwhile, in the squared circle John was continuing his quest to win the U.S. Championship. He accomplished this on the November 16, 2004, edition of *Smackdown!* He defeated Carlito, the Caribbean Cool, to win the U.S. Championship title for the third time. All along, he was using freestyle rap to entertain fans and intimidate foes.

After regaining the title, John unveiled a custom-made U.S. Championship belt that he had personally designed and ordered. The belt had a spinning center plate like the specially made decorative ornaments that spin inside car wheels and are popular with hip-hop fans. For John's belt, the spinning center plate had a red and blue background with two big block letters—*U.S.*—in white. The custom-made belt represented John's three true loves: wrestling, hip-hop, and the United States of America.

⟫ PURSUING THE WORLD CHAMPIONSHIP ⟪

Now John was focused on winning the WWE World Championship. That title was held by John "Bradshaw" Layfield, better known as JBL. Early in 2005, John was wrestling and defeating all the top contenders for the title, but JBL avoided wrestling him. That led to several verbal confrontations between John, JBL, and wrestlers who supported JBL, known as his "Cabinet members."

One of the members of JBL's Cabinet, Orlando Jordan, had lost to John in February 2005. But he managed to get a rematch with John on the March 3 edition of *Smackdown!* Orlando defeated John—but only with the help of other Cabinet members. However, the referee didn't see the interference, and Orlando was declared the winner and the new U.S. champion. A week later—on the March 10 edition of *Smackdown!*—Orlando and JBL destroyed John's special spinner belt. The feud between JBL, his Cabinet, and John continued to heat up.

Finally, John was given his world title shot at WrestleMania XXI, staged on April 3, 2005, in Los Angeles. In a difficult battle, during

John Cena strikes a pose with his WWE World Championship belt. John's road to the title ran through John "Bradshaw" Layfield—JBL. JBL did his best to avoid putting his title on the line against John. However, on April 3, 2005, the two finally faced off at WrestleMania XXI. John overcame JBL to gain the title.

which John escaped from several submission holds, John trapped JBL in the FU hold and then pinned him. John was the new WWE world champion.

⇒ A WORLD CHAMPIONSHIP BELT ⇐

To celebrate his victory, John had a new spinner belt made—this time with the World Championship logo in the middle. The new World Championship spinner belt that John created had more gold and diamonds than the traditional World Championship belt that

John takes time out from signing autographs to pose for a photo with a fan. After capturing the WWE World Championship title in April 2005, John became a crossover sensation. He released a new music video and a CD, *You Can't See Me.* He also made numerous appearances on television shows.

JBL had worn when he was champ. John said he wanted to give the belt more shine.

In an interview with *WWE Smackdown!* magazine, John talked about the new belt:

> **"The U.S. [Championship belt] got [quite] a reaction. I really wanted to take the WWE to another level. When I finally got my hands on [that belt], I really wanted to do something special with it."**

For John, the WWE Championship belt was the top trophy in the WWE. To give the new belt a proper introduction, John unveiled it on the April 14, 2005, edition of *Smackdown!* He had the custom-made spinner belt lowered into the ring from the ceiling as the crowd cheered.

Just a few weeks later, John's new music video premiered on the May 5 edition of *Smackdown!* The *Bad, Bad Man* music video **parodied** the culture of the 1980s. The song was also on John's CD, which was released five days later.

From mid-2005 through the following fall, John was secretly working on a new submission move. He debuted it in late November in a title match against Kurt Angle and Chris Masters. Called the STFU (Stepover Toehold Sleeper), the move is designed to force an opponent to submit quickly.

Riding a wave of popularity, John was asked to make many guest appearances. One, as a presenter on the 2005 Teen Choice Awards, teamed him with his one-time idol Hulk Hogan. John and the Hulkster worked out a skit in which they pretended to get into a fight during their presentation. The audience loved it.

Things were going great for John, who attained his goal of becoming WWE champion. But in professional wrestling another battle always looms. John had to continue working hard in order to fend off challengers for his title.

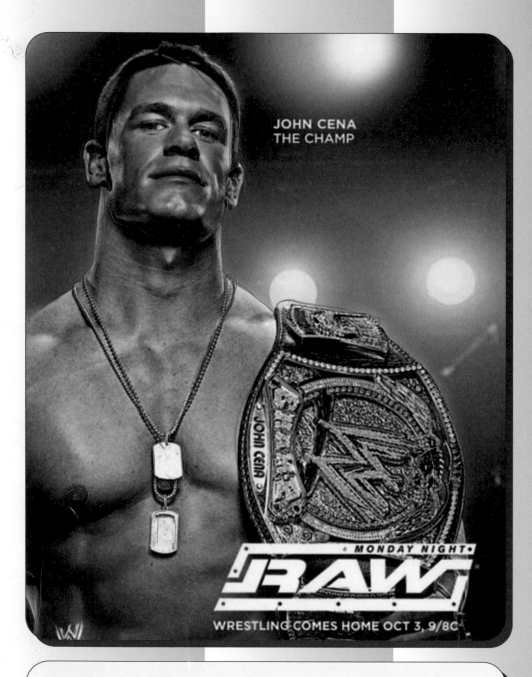

JOHN CENA
THE CHAMP

MONDAY NIGHT

RAW

WRESTLING COMES HOME OCT 3, 9/8C

The champ is featured on this ad for WWE's popular *Monday Night RAW* program. In 2005 John Cena moved from the *Smackdown!* to the *RAW* division. There he faced challengers such as Triple H, Shawn Michaels, Chris Masters, Kane, and Carlito—all of whom were itching to take away his title.

Being the Best

KURT ANGLE WANTED THE WWE CHAMPIONSHIP title. So did Chris Jericho. And JBL wanted to win the title back. Now that John was WWE champion, challengers for the coveted title belt were lining up in droves. John took on all comers, and hardly any major wrestling events were staged without him.

During his reign as WWE champ in 2005, he was drafted by *RAW* from *Smackdown!* The WWE has three divisions, or brands—*Smackdown!*, *RAW*, and *ECW* (Extreme Championship Wrestling, a league the WWE purchased in 2001). The draft rotates wrestlers between brands to keep the divisions fresh, competitive, and interesting. Unless there is an interdivision event or a battle for the overall WWE Championship, wrestlers usually take on challengers only from within their own division.

Since he first came to the WWE in 2001, John had always been with *Smackdown!* Now he would be battling wrestlers in *RAW*, including Triple H. In the first major pay-per-view WWE special of

2006, New Year's Resolution, John battled five men in a championship match in the Elimination Chamber. If any of the five—Kane, Shawn Michaels, Kurt Angle, Chris Masters, or Carlito—defeated him, John would lose the title.

➤ A WIN, THEN A QUICK LOSS ◄

John beat all five, but after the Elimination Chamber match, Edge entered the ring and cashed in his Money in the Bank contract. A Money in the Bank contract guarantees the holder a WWE Championship match whenever the owner of the contract demands it. An exhausted John Cena had to battle a well-rested Edge right at that moment.

In a short match, Edge defeated John and won the WWE title. John had held the title for 280 days. However, on January 29, just three weeks after losing the title, he battled Edge again in a Royal Rumble.

CROSS-CURRENTS

To find out how long some other great wrestling champions have held their titles, read "Reigning Champs." Go to page 54. ▶▶

He got Edge in an STFU hold and defeated him to recapture the WWE Championship.

John defeated Edge again nearly a month later in a Cage Match to retain the Championship. In WrestleMania XXII, on April 2, 2006, John successfully defended his belt against former WWE champion Triple H. Over the next months, John defended his title against both Edge and Triple H in a number of bouts.

➤ A WELL-KNOWN FACE ◄

John was becoming a recognizable face. As a result, he was asked to make appearances, to give interviews, and to cheer up sick children through the Make-A-Wish Foundation. John happily agreed to meet as many youngsters as possible. He also made numerous appearances on TV talk shows and gave interviews whenever he could.

John was thrilled to be interviewed for a cover story in the November 2006 issue of *Flex*. Some of the best bodybuilders in the world have been on the cover of that magazine, and as a youngster John used to staple *Flex* covers to the wall of his room. John told WWE.com:

> **66When the people from *Flex* say, 'Hey man, we want you on the cover,' that's a real good reward for always having to go to the gym.99**

John Cena shared the cover of *Pro Wrestling Illustrated*'s July 2007 issue with, among others, Donald Trump. John may have been the reigning WWE world champion, but Trump was more famous still. A billionaire real-estate developer and casino operator, Trump also had his own reality TV show, *The Apprentice*.

John also appeared on many major television shows. These included *Jimmy Kimmel Live*, *Late Night with Conan O'Brien*, *The Big Idea with Donnie Deutsch*, *Larry King Live*, *Mad TV*, *Good Day New York*, and ESPN's *Cold Pizza*.

≫ DEFENDING HIS TITLE ≪

Back in the ring, John was still defending his title, as well as defeating opponents in nontitle matches. On May 22, John bested Chris Masters in a nontitle match, but Rob Van Dam of the *ECW* informed him that he was cashing in his Money in the Bank contract. Van Dam

John Cena battles his nemesis Edge, who played a major role in John's losing the WWE World Championship title. On June 11, 2006, John was defending his title against Van Dam in a match in New York City when Edge sidled up ringside and hit John from behind. Stunned by the blow, John was easy prey for Van Dam.

challenged John for the WWE Championship on June 11 at One Night Stand in New York City, an annual pay-per-view wrestling event.

In the match, both men delivered heavy blows, but Van Dam won the match when Edge came ringside and hit John from behind without the referee seeing the blow. Van Dam then pinned John for the controversial win. Two weeks later, Edge defeated Van Dam to capture the WWE Championship for the second time.

John continued to battle Edge to win the title back. But every time Edge started to lose a match, he would deliberately do something to get himself disqualified. Losing a match through a disqualification does not result in losing the title. Finally, a match was set up for the annual SummerSlam in August. The WWE made Edge agree that if he got disqualified in this match, he would lose the match *and* the title.

SummerSlam was held in John's hometown of West Newbury, Massachusetts, with John heavily favored to win. But Edge was up to his old tricks. When he saw that the referee was distracted, he hit John with a foreign object. John fell to the mat and was pinned.

John tried unsuccessfully to get a rematch. Finally the WWE agreed to give John one more chance to defeat Edge if John would agree to leave *RAW* forever if he lost the match. John agreed, and the Championship match was set up for September at a major event called Unforgiven, held in Edge's hometown of Toronto.

This time John prevailed. Using his signature FU finishing move, John pinned Edge and won the Championship for the third time.

➣ BIG-SCREEN DEBUT ➤

A month later, John's movie *The Marine* was released. In line with *The Marine*, John started changing his image. Gone were hip-hop and throwback jerseys. Now John was wearing camouflage shorts and saluting the audience. He told WWE.com:

> **❝To be honest with you, I have a lot of respect for the armed services and what they stand for, their codes of discipline, regimen. And that pretty much fits the routine of the gym. You have to have discipline; you have to have a regimen.❞**

The Marine got a great deal of publicity and brought in $7 million in its first week. But John wasn't ready to retire from wrestling to pursue a movie career. He wanted to do both. The pro wrestling champ told the *Baltimore Sun*:

> **"I really don't ever intend to leave wrestling. Sports entertainment has provided me with a great life and is something that I really do have a lot of passion for. I'm going to go full-steam ahead with sports entertainment and full-steam ahead with Hollywood."**

After defeating Edge at Unforgiven, John held on to the title for a while. Again he successfully defended it against foes like Umaga and Randy Orton. In January 2007, John and Shawn Michaels unexpectedly teamed up and defeated Edge and Randy Orton to win the WWE Tag Team title. Now John held the two most treasured titles in the WWE.

⟫ A TROUBLED DUO ⟪

John and Shawn Michaels were a very successful Tag Team combo. They successfully defended their title against teams like the Under-taker and Batista; Lance Cade and Trevor Murdoch; Mercury and Nitro; and Shelton Benjamin and Charlie Haas. But John and Michaels also had very successful individual careers, and the fans could tell that the two didn't trust each other. Things got worse when the two battled each other for the WWE Championship title in WrestleMania XXIII on April 1, 2007.

John won the match when he got Michaels in a submission hold. A day later, in the second of two Tag Team Battles Royal, Michaels turned on John and threw him over the top rope and out of the ring. If one team member is thrown out of the ring over the top rope, it eliminates the team from the competition. The pair lost the Tag Team Championship that night to the Hardy Boys, and Shawn Michaels and John Cena went their separate ways.

John still held the WWE Championship. He was challenged by the Great Khali, a massive man who stands 7'3" tall and weighs 420 pounds. The Great Khali was one of John's largest opponents

CROSS-CURRENTS

To learn more about John's charitable work outside the wrestling ring, read "Always Ready to Help Others." Go to page 55. ▶▶

Semper Fi: John Cena poses with U.S. Marines and family members at Camp Pendleton, October 3, 2006. The occasion was the premiere of *The Marine*. Camp Pendleton, located near San Diego, California, is the base for approximately 35,000 active-duty Marines. It is the busiest military base in the country.

ever. On May 20, 2007, at the annual Judgment Day WWE event, John battled the Great Khali and bested him with an STFU hold.

A rematch was scheduled for June at One Night Stand, and John managed to pin the big man, becoming the first person in the WWE to pin the Great Khali. John wrestled at a feverish pace for the rest of 2007, earning his reputation as the hardest worker in professional wrestling.

⇉ A CAREER-THREATENING INJURY ⇇

But John's relentless pace caught up with him on October 1, 2007, when he tore his pectoral muscle in a match against Ken Kennedy.

In 2008 Gillette enlisted John Cena for an ad campaign promoting the company's new Fusion Phenom razor. Gillette, which is a sponsor of NASCAR, had John film a series of commercials with top drivers. This was a special thrill for John, who is a longtime fan of auto racing.

Because he could not defend the Championship title, the WWE took it away from him.

John's injury put his career in doubt. He had surgery the next day to repair the injury. Next came a period of intense rehabilitation. Doctors felt that John might be able to return to wrestling in about a year. John drew on his outstanding work ethic to accelerate his recovery.

Once his **incision** healed, John worked eight hours a day at his rehab. He told the *Miami Herald*: "It comes down to how much I want to hustle and be strong again." Amazingly, John was ready to get back in the ring again by the end of January, just four months after his injury. On January 27, 2008, he wrestled in a 30-man Royal Rumble. He won the match, eliminating Triple H to seal the victory. Several weeks later John triumphed over Randy Orton.

In early February, John also announced that he would start filming his next movie, titled *12 Rounds*, later in the month. As in *The Marine*, he would do many of his own stunts.

CROSS-CURRENTS
For some information about the roles of heroes and villains in pro wrestling, read "Heel Versus Face." Go to page 55.

⟫ READY FOR WRESTLEMANIA XXIV ⟪

Stunned wrestling fans soon found out that John would be strong enough to participate in WrestleMania XXIV on March 30, 2008, in Orlando. John was slated to wrestle the new WWE champion, Randy Orton, for the title. He lost that match but showed that he was completely healed and ready for more action. John was definitely back in fine form.

John's focus turned to regaining the WWE Championship title that was stripped from him. He knew it wouldn't be easy. But hard work has always been John Cena's hallmark.

The PWI 500

Every year since 1991, *Pro Wrestling Illustrated* magazine—recognized as the most authoritative publication in professional wrestling—issues a list of the top 500 wrestlers in the world. Known as the PWI 500, this list constitutes the undisputed ranking of professional wrestlers, including wrestlers in all leagues as well as independent brawlers. While other rankings are influenced by fan voting, the PWI 500 is based solely on input from the editors and writers of *Pro Wrestling Illustrated*. A team effort by these keen observers of the sport, the PWI 500 incorporates a series of objective measures, such as won-loss record, technical ability, influence on the sport, activity in the sport, level of competition, and success in matches against diverse competitors.

John Cena's rise up the PWI 500 has been nothing short of astonishing. By 2003, a year after he joined the WWE, John was ranked number 12 in the PWI 500. In 2004 he cracked the top 10, reaching number 7. He made it to the number 2 spot by 2005. In 2006 John reached

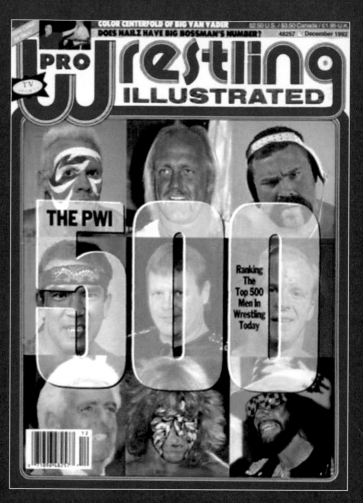

Pro Wrestling Illustrated*'s annual PWI 500 list is considered the authoritative ranking of professional wrestlers. The magazine's editors and writers evaluate wrestlers from all the leagues, as well as independent grapplers, for possible inclusion on the list of the world's top 500 performers. The PWI 500 has been compiled since 1991.*

number 1 on the PWI 500, and he remained at the top the following year as well.

(Go back to page 6.)

A Car Guy

When he wasn't watching wrestling as a kid, John Cena was fascinated by fast cars. Like his passion for professional wrestling, his love for cars carried over into adulthood. One of his hobbies outside the ring is building muscle cars. Muscle cars, which usually have two doors and are used for racing, are lightweight autos modified with big, powerful engines. The cars are custom-built from various parts of junked or used cars, so part of the fun is finding all the parts.

John began working on cars in his backyard at age 15. Today his collection of 20 cars includes a 1970 GTO, a 1970 Oldsmobile Cutlass, a 1971 Ford Torino, and a couple of newer models, such as a 2006 Ford GT—all muscle cars he built himself. He keeps his cars garaged. His main ride is a 1989 Jeep Wrangler, the first car he ever bought with his own money. The auto has racked up more than 175,000 miles, and John keeps it running strong. During an appearance on *Fast Cars & Superstars*, John said, "I'm absolutely a car guy."

(Go back to page 8.) ◀◀

"Absolutely a car guy": John Cena sits behind the wheel of a stock car as part of the ABC reality TV series Fast Cars & Superstars: The Gillette Young Guns Celebrity Race. *In the series, six NASCAR stars tutored 12 celebrity drivers, who competed against one another. John finished third in the competition, which football legend John Elway won.*

The Sport of Bodybuilding

Bodybuilding is a competitive sport that requires drive and determination. The early years of Western bodybuilding are considered to be between 1880 and 1930, but the sport actually started in India in the 11th century.

Arnold Schwarzenegger, governor of California, fields a reporter's question at a press conference. Before his entry into politics, the Austrian-born Schwarzenegger had been one of Hollywood's biggest stars—and before that, the world's premier bodybuilder. Schwarzenegger helped bring body-building into mainstream culture through his role in the 1977 documentary Pumping Iron.

To succeed in bodybuilding, a person must do constant weight training and follow a specific diet. Bodybuilders work for years to attain a physique that captures titles. Before becoming a professional wrestler, John Cena was an avid bodybuilder, working out every day at a gym. That **work ethic** served him well as he advanced within the ranks of professional wrestling.

Competitive bodybuilding got a big boost in 1977 when a documentary about the sport hit movie theaters. Titled *Pumping Iron*, the film featured Arnold Schwarzenegger and Lou Ferrigno. Many people took up bodybuilding after seeing that film, and both Schwarzenegger and Ferrigno went on to become famous.

Schwarzenegger, who held many international bodybuilding titles, became a movie star and governor of California. Ferrigno also won numerous bodybuilding titles before becoming an actor. He was best known for playing the title role in the TV series *The Incredible Hulk*. Ferrigno's physique was so good that Hollywood make-up artists did nothing to enhance his appearance as the Hulk, except paint him green so he resembled the comic book hero.

(Go back to page 13.) ◀◀

Like Son, Like Father

John Cena Sr., like his famous son, is involved in professional wrestling. A city assessor and justice of the peace, he moonlights as a wrestling manager under the moniker Johnny Fabulous. While John Sr. is by all accounts a mild-mannered gentleman, his alter ego is a conceited, inconsiderate wisecracker.

Around the time John Cena was embarking on a wrestling career, his dad, John Sr., answered an ad in a local newspaper. It was for a part-time job as a wrestling ring announcer for a regional professional wrestling association. When he applied for the job, the wrestling promoters were so impressed with his booming voice that they asked him to consider becoming a wrestling manager.

"It's more like a father following the son than the other way around," John Sr. said.

To be a wrestling manager, John Sr. had to develop a character. So he became Johnny Fabulous, a rich, arrogant wise guy. He had done

some acting at North Shore Community College in Beverly, Massachusetts, and he has been a wrestling fan ever since he was 10 years old. He also attended many wrestling matches at the Boston Garden. He drew on those experiences to create his character.

Johnny Fabulous appears at matches in the northeastern United States on weekends. He walks into the ring to a chorus of boos from fans. The boos let John Sr. know that he's doing his job.

During the week, Johnny Fabulous turns back into the mild-mannered John Cena Sr., the city assessor and justice of the peace in Methuen, Massachusetts. (Go back to page 14.) ◀◀

The Signature Move

Every professional wrestler has a signature, or finishing, move. The wrestler is usually identified with that particular move. Some signature moves may resemble others, but no matter how small the detail, there is always something that sets the move apart.

Many times wrestlers will name a signature move after themselves. Kurt Angle's move, for instance, is called the Angle Slam.

The signature move is used by a wrestler to finish off an opponent. John's signature moves are the FU and the STFU. A wrestler will practice a signature over and over again until another wrestler finds it almost impossible to defend against the move. If a signature move fails to be effective, the move may be revised or replaced altogether.

When wrestlers are in the ring, they try to do everything possible to avoid another wrestler's signature move, while trying to find an opening so they can use their own move. Wrestlers fear an opponent's signature move, though extremely good wrestlers can defend against a foe's move. True wrestling fans know most of the wrestlers' signature moves, and can tell when a wrestler is getting ready to use his.

Being on the receiving end of Big Show's signature move, the Abdominal Stretch, isn't a pleasant experience, as John Cena discovers here. Pro wrestlers will spend hours upon hours developing and perfecting a signature move. An effective signature move, deployed at the right time in a match, can be nearly impossible to resist.

(Go back to page 18.)

The Wrestler and the Hip-Hop Artist

When John Cena wanted to record his first CD, he turned to hip-hop veteran Tha Trademarc to show him the way. Tha Trademarc knew exactly what inspired John to write his rhymes and how he first came to love freestyle rap, because it was Tha Trademarc himself who first introduced John to hip-hop.

Tha Trademarc, whose real name is Marc Predka, is John's first cousin. Predka had been writing rhymes for more than 15 years by the time John was ready to record his first CD. Marc is two years older than John and grew up in Peabody, Massachusetts, not far from his cousin.

Marc would get all the new hip-hop releases, and the two would study the music and the artists for hours. While John and his brothers wrestled in their basement, Marc would write lyrics and record them in his own basement.

John and Marc got together and wrote "The Time Is Now," which became John's entrance theme every time he came into the ring. The song led to a recording deal with Columbia Records and was eventually released on John's CD *You Can't See Me.*

Both John and Marc continue to write hip-hop music. (Go back to page 22.) ◀◀

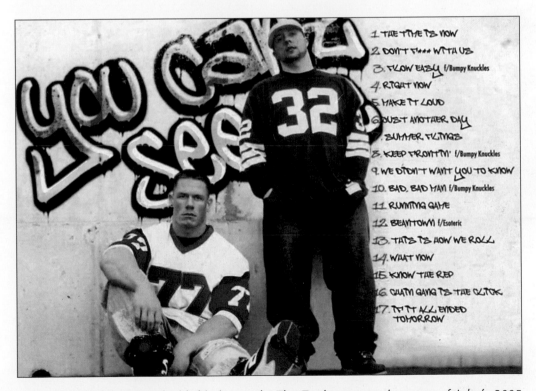

1. THE TIME IS NOW
2. DON'T F*** WITH US
3. FLOW EASY f/Bumpy Knuckles
4. RIGHT NOW
5. MAKE IT LOUD
6. JUST ANOTHER DAY
7. SUMMER FLINGS
8. KEEP FRONTIN' f/Bumpy Knuckles
9. WE DIDN'T WANT YOU TO KNOW
10. BAD, BAD MAN f/Bumpy Knuckles
11. RUNNING GAME
12. BEANTOWN f/Esoteric
13. THIS IS HOW WE ROLL
14. WHAT NOW
15. KNOW THE RED
16. CHAIN GANG IS THE CLICK
17. IF IT ALL ENDED TOMORROW

John Cena (left), pictured with hip-hop artist Tha Trademarc on the cover of John's 2005 rap CD, You Can't See Me. *Tha Trademarc—whose real name is Marc Predka and who is John's cousin—cowrote the single "The Time Is Now." John used the song as his wrestling theme music.*

WrestleMania

There is never an empty seat when Wrestle-Mania comes to town. WrestleMania is professional wrestling's biggest and most successful event. Held annually in March or April, Wrestle-Mania was started in 1985 in New York City's legendary Madison Square Garden. Featured was a Tag Team Championship match that pitted Hulk Hogan and Mr. T against Rowdy Rodney Piper and Paul Orndorff. Since then, the event has grown enormously; today it is watched by tens of thousands in person and millions on pay-per-view. A full card of wrestling's premier names is presented, with many major matches. Show business celebrities attend, and sometimes they play a role in the event.

WrestleMania is held in a different city each year. Host cities have included Boston, Philadelphia, New York City, Las Vegas, Los Angeles, Detroit, Seattle, Orlando, Hartford, and even Toronto, Canada. When WrestleMania III was staged in 1987, just outside Detroit in the Pontiac Silverdome, it drew a record crowd of more than 93,000 fans.

All of professional wrestling's biggest stars have appeared at WrestleMania through the years. Some launched their careers at WrestleMania; others saw their life-long careers come to a crushing end at this highly anticipated event. Titles have changed hands, feuds have been started, feuds have been settled, and professional wrestling has made history at the storied WrestleMania. (Go back to page 27.) ◄◄

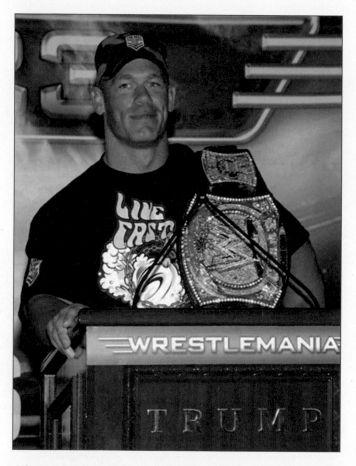

John Cena takes questions at a press conference about Wrestle-Mania XXIII, New York City, March 28, 2007. Four days later, at the 23rd edition of WrestleMania, held at Detroit's Ford Field, John would defend his WWE World Championship against Shawn Michaels. John prevailed, dispatching Michaels with his STFU move.

Wrestlers on the Big Screen

John Cena is not the first wrestler to make a movie. In 1982 Hulk Hogan gained a whole new audience when he appeared in *Rocky III* with Sylvester Stallone. Hogan played the part of—what else?—a professional wrestler. His character, named Thunderlips, battles boxer Rocky Balboa in a charity event.

The Hulkster has been in several other movies, including *No Holds Barred* in 1989 and *Mr. Nanny* in 1993. Since his crossover from wrestling to movies, other professional wrestlers have found it easier to land parts on the big screen.

The legendary and gigantic 7'4" pro wrestler André the Giant appeared in *Conan the Destroyer*, with Arnold Schwarzenegger, and *Micki and Maude*, both released in 1984. He also had a major role in 1987's *The Princess Bride*.

Wrestler–turned–wrestling announcer–turned–politician Jesse "the Body" Ventura also made movies. These included *Predator* (1987) and *Abraxas, Guardian of the Universe* (1991).

Dwayne "The Rock" Johnson started his film career with a small part in the 2001 movie *The Mummy Returns*. He followed this up with

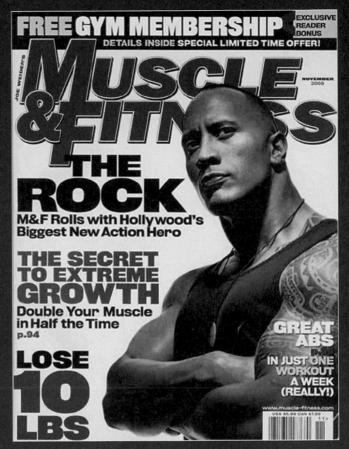

The cover of Muscle & Fitness *magazine's November 2003 issue featured Dwayne "The Rock" Johnson. The Rock is among a handful of pro wrestling stars who have tried their hands at movie acting. Others include Hulk Hogan, André the Giant, Jesse "the Body" Ventura. John Cena joined this group with* The Marine*.*

a major role in *The Scorpion King* (2002). The Rock has made many movies since then, and in 2004 he retired from professional wrestling to concentrate on his acting career.

(Go back to page 31.) ◀◀

Reigning Champs

Championship reigns in professional wrestling are much shorter today than they were years ago. Nevertheless, when it comes to the WWF, the WWWF (World Wide Wrestling Federation), and the WWE, John Cena fares very well in terms of total days holding the title.

Dating back to the early 1960s, legendary wrestler Bruno Sammartino held the title for a total of 4,040 days during two separate reigns. The great Hulk Hogan held the title for a combined 2,185 days during six different reigns.

As far as modern-day reigns go, John Cena has held the title longer than most of his peers. In fact, combining the total days a professional wrestler in today's ranks has held the title, only one wrestler—Triple H—had held the title longer than John.

During his three reigns as champion, John has held the title for a combined total of 793 days, sixth on the all-time list. Sammartino, Hogan, Bob Backlund, Pedro Morales, and Triple H are the only wrestlers who held the championship belt longer. Triple H had the title for a total of 877 days.

Triple H strikes an intimidating pose in this publicity photo. His success inside the ring is indisputable: among modern-day wrestlers, no one has reigned as WWE champion for a greater total time than Triple H. John Cena ranks second on the list.

The list of contemporary wrestlers whose reigns have been shorter than John's includes some of the biggest names in the industry, including Kurt Angle, The Rock, Steve Austin, Bret Hart, and Batista.

(Go back to page 38.)

Always Ready to Help Others

Once John Cena became a major professional wrestling star, he began to get requests to help people who were less fortunate. He jumped at the chance. One of his passions is working with the Make-A-Wish Foundation, an organization that grants the wishes of children with life-threatening illnesses. John granted 100 wishes in four years, helping sick youngsters all over the country.

The foundation recognized John's efforts by giving him a special commemorative plaque. Upon receiving the award, John told WWE.com: "I am honored to be part of a foundation that makes so many kids happy. It makes me feel good just to be a small piece of the puzzle."

John also volunteers his time to entertain American troops stationed in the United States and overseas. He considers the matches that the WWE stages for troops in Afghanistan and Iraq the biggest event of the year—bigger for him than WrestleMania.

In December 2007 John went on the WWE's tour to Tikrit in Iraq, even though he had hurt a pectoral muscle earlier in the year and was unable to wrestle. Determined not to let his injury stand in the way of boosting the troops' morale, he visited with military personnel, signed autographs, and lifted the soldiers' spirits.

(Go back to page 42.) ◀◀

Heel Versus Face

In professional wrestling a villain is referred to as a heel. A heel will break the rules, attack other wrestlers outside the ring, attack wrestlers when they aren't looking, use foreign objects in the ring, and antagonize the crowd. Heels are booed and disliked by the crowd.

A hero is referred to as a face. A face serves as a role model. He never cheats. He is well mannered and polite, he overcomes adversity, and he helps other wrestlers if they are victims of a sneak attack by heels. A face is cheered and revered by the fans.

A tweener is an unpredictable wrestler. Sometimes tweeners are good; other times they are evil. From one match to another, fans never know what to expect from a tweener.

Usually, good things happen to the face and bad things happen to the heel. Evil usually loses out in the end, though it may take some time for good to triumph. Some heels have even held titles in professional wrestling, but a face always wrestles the title away from him, winning fair and square—to the delight of the fans.

(Go back to page 45.) ◀◀

1977   Jonathan Felix Anthony Cena Jr. is born April 23 in West Newbury, Massachusetts.

1999   Graduates from Springfield College in Massachusetts with a degree in exercise physiology.

Goes to California and enrolls in Ultimate University to become a professional wrestler.

2000   Makes his professional wrestling debut with Ultimate Pro Wrestling (UPW).

2001   Signs a developmental contract with the WWF and is sent to Ohio Valley Wrestling.

2002   On June 27, makes his first television appearance for WWE on *Smackdown!* against Kurt Angle.

2003   Introduces his signature move, the Fireman's Carry PowerSlam, also known as the FU.

2004   Wins the WWE U.S. Championship in March, and starts his quest for the World Championship.

Unveils a custom-made U.S. Championship spinner belt in November.

Starts filming his first movie, *The Marine*, late in the year.

Is voted Most Popular Wrestler of the Year by readers of *Pro Wrestling Illustrated*.

2005   Wins the WWE World Championship for the first time, on April 3.

First rap CD, titled *You Can't See Me*, is released on May 10.

Is voted Most Popular Wrestler of the Year by readers of *Pro Wrestling Illustrated*.

2006   *The Marine* is released in October.

John Cena is voted Wrestler of the Year by readers of *Pro Wrestling Illustrated*.

Is ranked number one on the PWI 500.

2007   Tears his pectoral muscle during a match on October 1, and requires surgery.

Is voted Wrestler of the Year by readers of *Pro Wrestling Illustrated*.

Ranked number one on the PWI 500.

Voted Most Popular Wrestler of the Year by readers of *Pro Wrestling Illustrated*.

2008   Returns from his injury ahead of schedule and wins a 30-man Royal Rumble on January 27.

In February, starts filming the movie *12 Rounds*.

1999 NCAA Division III Football All-American

2000 UPW Championship

2001 Ohio Valley Wrestling Southern Tag Team Championship (with Rico Constantino)

2002 Ohio Valley Wrestling Heavyweight Championship

2004 U.S. Championship

2005 WWE Championship

2006 WWE Championship

2007 World Tag Team Championship (with Shawn Michaels)

John Cena's Championship Reigns
WWE U.S. Championship: Three Times
March 14, 2004–July 8, 2004
October 3, 2004–October 7, 2004
November 18, 2004–March 3, 2005

WWE Tag Team Championship, with Shawn Michaels
January 29, 2007–April 2, 2007

WWE World Championship: Three Times
April 3, 2005–January 8, 2006
January 29, 2006–June 11, 2006
September 17, 2006–October 2, 2007

Books

Caprio, Robert. *Are We There Yet? Tales from the Neverending Travels of WWE Superstars*. New York: Pocket Books, 2005.

Fritz, Brian, and Christopher Murray. *Between the Ropes: Wrestling's Greatest Triumphs and Failures*. Toronto: ECW Press, 2006.

Solomon, Brian. *WWE Legends*. New York: Pocket Books, 2006.

Wolff, Robert. *Bodybuilding 101: Everything You Need to Know to Get the Body You Want*. New York: McGraw-Hill, 2006.

Wrestling Annual: The Year in Review. Blue Bell, PA: Sports and Entertainment Publications, 2008.

Web Sites

http://www.wwe.com

The WWE's Web site includes updates on all of John Cena's matches and appearances, as well as biographical information and facts about his career.

http://www.pwi-online.com

The online site of *Pro Wrestling Illustrated* magazine, which covers all wrestling events and gives rankings.

http://www.imdb.com/find?s=all&q=john+cena&x=17&y=9

This page spotlights John Cena's movies (including entire cast credits) and includes a short biography.

http://www.music.aol.com/artist/john-cena/2210456

This music information site includes all the latest information on John Cena's CDs and his music career.

http://www.tv.com/john-cena/person/140009/biography.html

An entertainment site that contains a biography of John Cena as well as links to breaking stories about wrestling and entertainment ventures.

alleged—stated without offering proof.

aspiring—seeking to accomplish a goal.

charismatic—having magnetic charm or appeal.

coveted—highly sought-after.

embarked—made a start.

foray—an attempt at something, often outside one's regular field.

improvisational—referring to something done off the top of one's head or without practice.

incision—a cut made by a doctor during surgery.

moniker—a nickname.

parodied—made fun of through imitation.

pectoral muscle—either of two muscles in the chest that connect to the bones of the upper arm and the shoulder.

rehabilitation—exercises to regain strength and flexibility after an injury.

savvy—smart, shrewd, and well informed.

squared circle—an informal term for a wrestling ring.

taunts—mocking challenges or insults; challenging in a mocking or insulting manner.

work ethic—a belief that work is morally good and should be pursued.

Chapter 1

page 6 "I'm one that loves . . ." Kara A. Medalis, "It's FLEX Time for Cena," WWE.com, August 24, 2006. http://www.wwe.com/inside/news/archive/cenaflex

page 6 "What you see . . ." Telephone interview with John Cena Sr., March 25, 2008.

Chapter 2

page 11 "It's the only reason . . ." Telephone interview with John Cena Sr.

page 11 "If you would have told me . . ." Ibid.

page 12 "He made a Championship . . ." Ibid.

page 13 "Two things I remember about John . . ." Telephone interview with Mike DeLong, Springfield College football coach, March 25, 2008.

page 14 "Wrestling was always so secretive . . ." Kevin Eck, "WWE Champ Is a Triple Threat," *Baltimore Sun*, October 13, 2006. http://www.baltimoresun.com/sport/other/bal-cena101306.0.2594869.story

page 14 "He didn't tell me . . ." Telephone interview with John Cena Sr.

Chapter 3

page 21 "My character is me . . ." Sean Hyson, "John Cena: WWE's Smackdown! Superstar Raps about his Upcoming Movie, CD—and Life Outside the Ring," *Men's Fitness*, April 2005. http://findarticles.com/p/articles/mi_m1608/is_3_21/ai_n13504304/pg_1

page 25 "I'm not afraid to fail . . ." ibid.

Chapter 4

page 30 "John is a director's dream . . ." Benjamin Leszcz, "The Lord of the Ring," *Toro*, Winter 2006. http://www.toromagazine.ca/1006/johncena/index.html

page 30 "[John Cena] has a strong . . ." Evan Henerson, "Semper Fi: 'The Marine' Star & WWE Wrestling Champ Has Faith in His Future," *Los Angeles Daily News*, October 14, 2006. http//:www.wwe.com/superstars/raw/johncena/reviews/3481716

page 30 "I got about a month . . ." Kevin Eck, "WWE Champ Is a Triple Threat," *Baltimore Sun*, October 13, 2006. http://www.baltimoresun.com/sports/other/bal-cena101306,0,2594869.story

page 35 "The U.S. [Championship belt] got . . ." Brian Solomon, "The Champ's New Bling: Giving a Different Spin to the WWE Championship," *WWE Smackdown!*, June 2005. http://www.100megsfree4.com/wiawrestling/pages/wwf/cenawwebelt.htm

Chapter 5

page 38 "When the people from *Flex* . . ." Kara A. Medalis, "It's FLEX Time for Cena," WWE.com, August 24, 2006. http://www.wwe.com/inside/news/archive/cenaflex

page 41 "To be honest with you . . . " Ibid.

page 42 "I really don't ever intend . . ." Eck, "WWE Champ."

page 45 "It comes down to how . . ." Jim Varsallone, "Cena Misses Working," *Miami Herald,* November 14, 2007. http://nl.newsbank.com/nl-search/we/Archives?p_action=list&p_topdoc=31

Cross-Currents

page 49 "It's more like a father . . ." Telephone interview with John Cena Sr.

page 55 "I am honored to be part of a foundation . . ." Greg Adkins, "Cena Turns 100," WWE.com, March 29, 2008. http://www.wwe.com/shows/wrestlemania/exclusives/6753142

Achberger, Rick "Sign Guy," 7–8
André the Giant, 11, 53
Angle, Kurt, *16*, 18, *19*, *20*, 28, 35, 37, 38, 50, 54
Austin, Stone Cold Steve, 30, 54

Backlash 2003, 25
Batista, 8, 42, 54
Benjamin, Shelton, 42
Benoit, Chris, *20*, 25
Big Show, 27–28, 50
bodybuilding, *10*, 13, 14, 48
Bonito, John, 30
Booker T, *20*, 29, 30

Cade, Lance, 42
Carlito, the Caribbean Cool, 30, 32, *36*, 38
Carlson, Kelly, *7*, 30
Cena, Carol (mother), 11
Cena, Dan (brother), 11, 13
Cena, John
    awards won by, 6
    birth and childhood, 11–13
    and bodybuilding, *10*, 13, 14, 48
    and cars, 8, *44*, 47
    and the "Chain Gang," 22, *23*
    charity work, 8, 38, 55
    endorsements, 7, *44*
    and injuries, 8–9, 43, 45
    joins the WWE, 14–15
    and movies, 6, 30–32, 41–42, 45, 53
    nicknames, 14, 15, 19
    as Ohio Valley Wrestling champion, 15
    plays football at Springfield College, 13–14, 22

    and rapping, 6, 13, 20–23, *29*, 32, *34*, 51
    on *RAW,* 36–38
    signature moves of, 22, *23*, 28, 34, 35, 38, 41, 43, 50
    on *Smackdown!,* *16*, 18–19, 21–22, 28, 30, 32, 35, 36–37
    and spinning championship belts, *4*, 32, 34–35
    and television shows, 7–8, 40, 47
    and U.S. troops, 8, *9*, 41, *43*, 55
    as WWE U.S. Champion, 27–29
    as WWE World Champion, *4*, 5, 9, *33*, 34–38, 40–43, 45
    as WWE World Tag Team champion, 6, 8, 42
Cena, John, Sr. (father), 6, 11–12, 14, 49
Cena, Matt (brother), 11, 13
Cena, Sean (brother), 11, 13
Cena, Steve (brother), 11, 13
"Chain Gang," 22, *23*
charity work, 8, 38, 55
Constantino, Rico, 15

Deal or No Deal, 7–8
DeLong, Mike, 13

ECW (Extreme Championship Wrestling), 37
    See also World Wrestling Entertainment (WWE)
Edge, *20*, 38, *40*, 41, 42
Extreme Makeover: Home Edition, 8

F5 (signature move), 22, 25
Family Feud, 8
Fast Cars & Superstars, 8, 47
Ferrigno, Lou, 48
FU (signature move), 22, *23*, 28, 34, 41, 50

Great Khali, 42–43

Haas, Charlie, 42
Hardy Boys, 42
Hogan, Hulk, 11, *12*, 35, 52, 53, 54

JBL (John "Bradshaw" Layfield), 32–35, 37
Jericho, Chris, 18, 37
Johnson, Dwayne "The Rock," 53, 54
Jordan, Orlando, 32

Kane, *36*, 38
Kennedy, Ken, 8, 43

Lashley, Bobby, 8
Lesnar, Brock, *20*, 22, 25
Leydon, Joe, *31*

The Marine, 6, *7*, 30–32, 41–42, *43*
Massaro, Ashley, 8
Masters, Chris, 35, *36*, 38, 40
McMahon, Stephanie, 22
McMahon, Vince, 17–18
Mercury, 42
Michaels, Shawn, 6, 8, *36*, 38, 42, 52
"Mr. P." *See* Cena, John
Murdoch, Trevor, 42

Numbers in ***bold italics*** refer to captions.

Nitro, 42
No Mercy, 29

Ohio Valley Wrestling (OVW), 15
Orton, Randy, 42, 45

Pro Wrestling Illustrated, 6, **39**, 46
"Prototype." *See* Cena, John
PWI 500, 6, 46

RAW, 36–38
    Rebellion Tour, **20**, 21
        See also World Wrestling Entertainment (WWE)
Royal Rumble, 25, 27, 38, 45

Sammartino, Bruno, 54
Schwarzenegger, Arnold, 48, 53
Smackdown!, **16**, 18–19, 21–22, 28, 30, 32, 35, 36–37
        See also World Wrestling Entertainment (WWE)

Springfield College, 13–14, 22
Stallone, Sylvester, 53
STFU (Stepover Toehold Sleeper), 35, 38, 43, 50

Tha Trademarc (Mark Predka), 32, 51
Triple H, **36**, 37, 38, 45, 54
12 Rounds, 45

Ultimate Pro Wrestling (UPW), 14
Ultimate University, 14
Ultimate Warrior, 11
Umaga, 42
Undertaker, 18, 42

Van Dam, Rob, 40–41
Ventura, Jesse "the Body," 53

World Wrestling Entertainment (WWE), **4**, 5–6, 25, 52, 54–55
    RAW division, 20–21, 36–37, 40–41

Smackdown! division, 18–19, 21–22, 28, 30, 32, 34–35
    "Tribute to the Troops" tours, **9**, 55
    as the World Wrestling Federation (WWF), 14–15, 17
        See also The Marine; WrestleMania
World Wrestling Federation (WWF). *See* World Wrestling Entertainment (WWE)
WrestleMania
    XX, 25, 27–28, 52
    XXI, 32–33
    XXII, 38
    XXIII, 42
    XXIV, 45
        See also World Wrestling Entertainment (WWE)
Wrestler of the Year award, 6

You Can't See Me (album), 6, **29**, 32, **34**, 35, 51

Robert Grayson is an award-winning former daily newspaper reporter whose assignments included feature stories on professional wrestling. He has also had articles published in the *New York Yankees* magazine, *NBA Hoop* magazine, and *Sports Collectors Digest*, among many other sports, entertainment, and lifestyle publications. An avid cat lover, he has written a series of features about cats and dogs in the movies for many animal companion magazines and Web sites.

PICTURE CREDITS

page

1: Mark Von Holden/WireImage
4: Michael Wright/WWE/PRMS
7: WWE Films/FilmMagic
9: U.S. DoD/NMI
10: Mark Von Holden/WireImage
12: Kevin Mazur/WireImage
15: J. McCabe/PRMS
16: WWE/PRMS
19: WWE/PRMS
20: WWE/PRMS
23: WWE/PRMS
24: Michael Wright/WWE/PRMS
26: Michael Wright/WWE/PRMS
28: WWE/NMI
29: WWE/PRMS
31: Vince Valituti/WWE Films/FilmMagic

33: Scott Brinegar/WWE/PRMS
34: Holly Sharpe/CIC Photos
36: WWE/USA Network/NMI
39: Wrestling Illustrated/NMI
40: WWE/PRMS
43: U.S. DoD/NMI
44: Gillette/NMI
46: Wrestling Illustrated/NMI
47: Gillette/NMI
48: Roll Call Photos
49: MWF/PRMS
50: USAF/DoD/NMI
51: Columbia Records/WWE/NMI
52: Jamie McCarthy/WireImage
53: Muscle & Fitness/NMI
54: Rich Freeda/WWE/PRMS

Front cover: WWE/PRMS